POIRET

1913   Chiffon and satin evening dresses designed for Poiret by Erté.

POIRET

A RIZZOLI PAPERBACK

Rizzoli
NEW YORK

ACKNOWLEDGEMENTS
We should like to thank Michael Pruskin for the loan of material for Plate 11. All other
illustrations are from the archives of Academy Editions.

First published in the United States of America in 1979 by

RIZZOLI INTERNATIONAL PUBLICATIONS, INC.
712 Fifth Avenue/New York 10019

Copyright © 1979 Academy Editions London

Library of Congress Catalog Card Number 79-64759
ISBN 0-8478-0247-7

Printed and bound in Hong Kong

INTRODUCTION

Paris, at the turn of the century, was a city of cultural ferment, attracting enthusiastic young artists and designers from all over Europe. Paul Poiret, however, was a native of the city and grew up immersed in the traditions of French couture and well aware of the nature of the fashionable woman he was later to dress. He was surrounded also by the new movements in art and literature which attempted to sever the links with the previous century and, in particular, with the excesses of Art Nouveau. Inspired by this spirit of change, Poiret brought about a revolution in fashion, introducing the simple, elegant lines of Art Deco style and illustration.

Born in Paris in 1879, Poiret showed from an early age an interest in colour and design combined with a vivid imagination. Using only those resources readily available his first inventions ranged from garden fountains to the crushing of petals to make perfume. It was only during an enforced apprenticeship with an umbrella maker that Poiret began seriously to experiment with fabric and patterns, taking home scraps of material and pinning them to a small wooden mannequin. Recognition of his obvious talent came in 1898 when Madame Cheruit, one of the leading designers of the time, accepted some of his sketches and subsequently, despite much parental opposition, he was allowed to work for the Grand Gentleman of Fashion himself, Jacques Doucet. Doucet was Poiret's idol and encouraged the young man by giving him the most demanding commissions, to which his creative imagination readily responded. He was not to find such tolerant mentors in the Worth brothers for whom he worked after his National Service. Finding Poiret's designs too original for their more conservative customers they tended to suppress his ideas and curb his growing enthusiasm. And so, in 1903, after only four years experience in the Paris fashion houses, Poiret decided to open his own premises.

Parisian women of the early 1900s were still suffering beneath the constraints of the corset which gave them the stern, exaggerated line of an S-bend. Poiret believed the inherent mystery and charm of a woman should be evoked by suggestion and understatement and this led to his first innovation — the removal of the corset and its replacement by the more supple girdle. This emancipation of the body altered the female silhouette and occasioned not only a new way of designing clothes but of illustrating them.

Poiret held that the roles of artist and designer should compliment one another in reflecting changes in society and that fashion, like art, should be constantly progressing. Having always been receptive to new movements such as Fauvism and Symbolism, Poiret wished to further this essential link by associating closely with other artists.

The first move in this direction came in 1908, when, because of the success of his new designs reminiscent of the sensuous Empire line, Poiret commissioned Paul Iribe to illustrate his clothes with a view to reproducing them in an album. The artist is mentioned in Poiret's autobiography, *My First Fifty Years,* as having 'all but swooned' in his amazement and pleasure at being called upon to work with such beautiful designs. This affinity with Poiret's work enabled Iribe to produce the first album of its kind to show the close relationship between the clothes and their illustrator — thus setting a precedent for future Art Deco illustrators.

The collection entitled *Les Robes de Paul Poiret,* (Plates 1-8), emphasises the vivid colours of Poiret's dresses by placing them against the traditional monochrome background of earlier engravings. In this way, the detail of the furniture enhances the simplicity and grace of his designs. Even the treatment of the models is strikingly innovative in that Iribe looked to Japanese prints for the mystery and aura of confidence with which he imbued his figures.

Among the many famous women who flocked to the couturier house of Paul Poiret were the actress Réjane and the Countess Greffulhe, leader of Parisian high society. By now his reputation was not only limited to Paris for the name Poiret was recognised and revered all over Europe and America by fashionable women. To increase his sphere of influence, Poiret and his wife embarked on a European tour in 1911, venturing as far as St. Petersburg. There, as well as attracting a large clientele, his designs caught the eye of a young artist, Romain de Tirtoff (later known as Erté) who came to Paris the following year and became Poiret's assistant designer.

The success, both of his clothes and of Iribe's work in immortalizing them, prompted Poiret to consider a second album. This time the commission fell to Georges Lepape, a little known artist whose talent Poiret recognised and encouraged. In *Les Choses de Paul Poiret,* published in 1911, Lepape continued the style introduced by Iribe but treated the background in a different way, dispelling once and for all the last vestiges of traditional illustration. In this work (Plates 9-16) the popular high-waisted dress is still present but with an even narrower 'hobble' skirt and a distinct oriental influence. The arrival of the Ballets Russes in Paris in 1909 and Léon Bakst's costume designs heralded a new craze which Poiret anticipated by the introduction of the turban, the tunic and the pantaloon gown in rich exotic prints from the Middle East. In spite of the restrictive 'hobble' dress, Lepape understood the intrinsic practicality behind Poiret's exotic designs and illustrated four different costumes based on the pantaloon showing its potential for greater freedom of movement for women (Plate 16).

This attraction to the Orient embraced not only fashion but many other branches of the decorative arts and Poiret was quick to perceive another link that could be established between these different fields. To this end, in 1911, he launched two new projects: Rosine, a perfume company and Martine, an interior design workshop. Poiret's scents, based on exotic spices and herbs, were the perfect compliment to his designs and following their success he introduced soaps and cosmetics. The Martine school, on the other hand, encouraged its students to create not only designs for furnishing fabrics and wallpapers but printed silks and taffetas for Poiret's dresses.

The success of these ventures allowed Poiret to indulge even more in the pleasures of pre-war Paris. The trend towards lavish parties and costly gowns in which to attend them was the privilege of the wealthy elite, under the fashionable leadership of the Poirets. Fashion became big business and the need arose to publish more magazines commenting on fashion and advertising the latest styles. Concurrent with this mood was renewed interest in the *pochoir* method of printing and the presence in Paris at that time of a large number of talented illustrators whose excellent work was ideally suited to this process of reproduction. In 1912, therefore, several new magazines appeared using the *pochoir* technique, the most representative and successful being the *Gazette du Bon Ton* under the direction of Lucien Vogel.

Vogel's team of illustrators included Lepape whose career had been launched by the success of *Les Choses de Paul Poiret.* He contributed regularly to the magazine until its merger with *Vogue* in 1925 but most of his illustrations of Poiret gowns were executed between 1912 and 1915. These designs show a continuing interest in oriental styles and, in particular, in the tunic which features strongly in these early illustrations (Plates 17-21). André Marty took over where Lepape left off and after the war became Poiret's most prolific illustrator in the *Gazette du Bon Ton.* Less extreme than either Edouard Benito or Charles Martin, both strongly influenced by the Cubists, Marty's style suited the designs Poiret was producing in the early 20s.

Maintaining always that the universal need to conform and the mistrust of anything new was at variance with the concept of fashion, Poiret continued after the First World War to produce original and unusual designs. He drew inspiration from the past, adapting medieval, renaissance and eighteenth century styles to contemporary, exotic fabrics (Plates 22-27). What Poiret failed to grasp was that the war had had a profound effect on women and their life-styles. They had assumed a more responsible and independent role in society and were not prepared to return to the cumbersome tight waists and full skirts that Poiret was advocating. Their new-found freedom was symbolised by shorter hem-lines and light-weight fabrics which showed off their slimmer, elegant silhouette. The deprivations of the war necessitated an economy and simplicity of dress which Poiret adamantly opposed by introducing yet more lavish and costly materials.

If it was his extravagant life-style that made Poiret's reputation before the war, it was his continuing excellence in design and choice of fabric that led to his downfall. The excessive tastes which made his clothes so unsuitable were also reflected in some of his business ventures. An example of this was the conversion of his garden into an exclusive night club, L'Oasis, (Plate 29) which proved too refined for the increasingly bohemian tastes of the fashionable young Parisians. Poiret himself saw the designer as 'an artist in luxury' and not only lived according to that tenet but continued to design expensive clothes long after the demise of the ostentatious era he had epitomised.

In the early 20s he accepted many commissions to design costumes for the theatre, which all proved to be an enormous success but harmed his image as a designer of contemporary fashion. Yet he continued to be represented in the monthly periodicals, particularly *Art, Goût, Beauté* which first appeared in 1920. In these later illustrations there is a much stronger distinction to be seen between day dresses and evening gowns. The former have become more functional and leisure conscious — a trend Poiret predicted as early as 1908 when he declared that a dress which could not be worn in the street as well as the drawing room was useless. The evening gown, on the other hand, is still as lavish as any he produced before the war, made up in satins, silks, lamés and furs (Plates 35-40).

Gradually, the *Gazette* which was still the most influential magazine, illustrated Poiret's designs less and less, indicating a slight waning of his popularity. It was not that his clothes were ugly, they were simply too original; the product, as the *Gazette* said, of a man *'qui ne crée rien de prévu ou qui puisse être destiné à tout le monde'*, (who revels in the unexpected, producing designs that few people can wear). He continued, however, to exercise his innovative mind and in 1922 commissioned a young photographer, Man Ray, to present his collection in a different medium.

In 1925 the perfect occasion arose for Poiret to make a comeback when Paris held its great Art Deco exhibition, which the organisers admitted could only have been mounted because of Poiret's important contribution to the arts. Unfortunately, the extravagant habits which he had formed early in life, coupled with his fertile imagination, involved him in schemes which, while showing the world that Paul Poiret was still very much a creative genius, ruined him financially.

From 1925 until 1929 Poiret's business was entirely in the hands of a board of directors established to control its rapidly deteriorating financial position and finally, in the summer of 1925, they closed the fashion house altogether. Yet in 1931 Poiret stepped back into the limelight with a new collection financed by a firm of silk manufacturers but which once again proved too lavish for Europeans in the grip of the Depression.

From then on, as the condition of his finances worsened, so too did his health. He died in 1944, bankrupt and forgotten by the designers whose styles, which still influence us today, evolved out of his foresight and imagination.

The illustrations selected in this book span the most productive and successful years of Poiret's career from 1908 to 1926. Where possible a description of the garment has been given to indicate some of the care and attention devoted to each creation and to underline Poiret's constant maxim of fashion — *'il convient qu'elle soit le privilège d'une élite'*, (that it should be the privilege of the elite).

Nicole Thornton

1

1908
Three gowns.
Paul Iribe
Les Robes de Paul Poiret

2

1908
Three coats.
Paul Iribe
Les Robes de Paul Poiret

3

1908
Dress.
Paul Iribe
Les Robes de Paul Poiret

4

1908
Two gowns.
Paul Iribe
Les Robes de Paul Poiret

5

1908
Two gowns.
Paul Iribe
Les Robes de Paul Poiret

6

1908
Evening gown.
Paul Iribe
Les Robes de Paul Poiret

7

1908
Three gowns.
Paul Iribe
Les Robes de Paul Poiret

8

1908
Two evening gowns.
Paul Iribe
Les Robes de Paul Poiret

9

1911
Day dress.
Georges Lepape
Les Choses de Paul Poiret

10

1911
Fur trimmed gown.
Georges Lepape
Les Choses de Paul Poiret

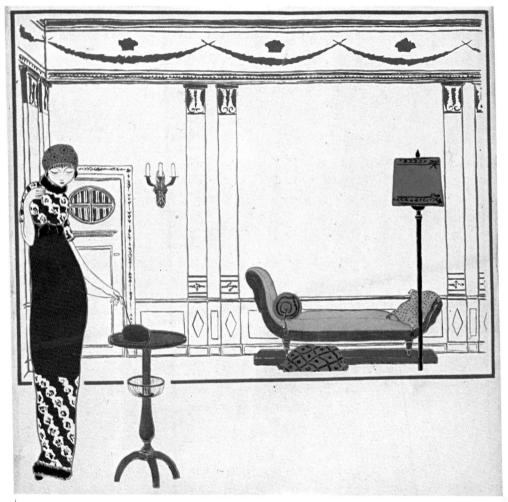

11

1911
Gown and two fur trimmed capes.
Georges Lepape
Les Choses de Paul Poiret

Georges Lepape

12

1911
Gown.
Georges Lepape
Les Choses de Paul Poiret

13

1911
Turban.
Georges Lepape
Les Choses de Paul Poiret

14

1911
Two evening gowns.
Georges Lepape
Les Choses de Paul Poiret

15

1911
Fur trimmed gown.
Georges Lepape
Les Choses de Paul Poiret

16

CELLES DE DEMAIN
1911
Four pantaloon dresses.
Georges Lepape
Les Choses de Paul Poiret

17

LASSITUDE
1912
Soft white velvet tunic under a shorter
tunic of black tulle embroidered with flowers.
Georges Lepape
Gazette du Bon Ton

georges lepape   12.

18

SERAIS-JE EN AVANCE?
1912
Theatre coat of yellow silk, trimmed with
skunk fur, a blue/green satin lining and
embroidered clasp.
Georges Lepape
Gazette du Bon Ton

19

L'ARBRE EN FLEURS
1913
White crêpe dress worn under a lawn tunic
and straw hat trimmed with black satin and
flowers.
Georges Lepape
Gazette du Bon Ton

20

LE LYS ROUGE
1914
Evening gown with gold tunic and
green and black embroidered skirt.
Simone Puget
Gazette du Bon Ton

21

LA ROBE BLANCHE
1914
White dress with tiered skirt.
Jean-Louis Boussingault
Gazette du Bon Ton

JLB

22

DANAE
1914
Velvet evening cape.
Charles Martin
Gazette du Bon Ton

23

MIRAGE
1920
Evening gown with turquoise tulle
skirt and embroidered silver lamé bodice.
Mario Simon
Gazette du Bon Ton

25

LE JARDIN DE L'INFANTE
1920
Evening gown of white satin edged in black
satin over a white gauze petticoat.
Charles Martin
Gazette du Bon Ton

26

RELATION
1921
Coat of green bouclé wool.
Charles Martin
Gazette du Bon Ton

27

LES PLAISIRS DE LA CAMPAGNE
1921
Tulle and taffeta dress decorated
with ribbons and fabric flowers.
André Marty
Gazette du Bon Ton

28

PENSE-T-IL A MOI?
1921
Printed silk dress with organdi collar and
hem.
André Marty
Gazette du Bon Ton

29

A L'OASIS OU LA VOUTE PNEUMATIQUE
1921
Red crêpe tunic embroidered with
golden ears of corn, worn
over a shimmering gold dress.
André Marty
Gazette du Bon Ton

30

VOILA LE PRINTEMPS
1922
Royal blue and purple dress for spring.
André Marty
Gazette du Bon Ton

31

LA BICHE APPRIVOISEE
1922
Printed silk dress with crêpe sleeves and
organdi frills on the cuffs and neckline.
André Marty
Gazette du Bon Ton

A.E.MARTY·1921·

32

AU REVOIR, MON AMOUR
1922
Black and white crêpe dress with silk belt and
tassles.
Edouard Benito
Gazette du Bon Ton

33

1923
Two evening gowns.
Cover, *Art, Goût, Beauté*

Créations
PAUL POIRET

Art - Goût - Beauté

34

LA DERNIERE SEANCE OU LA CRITIQUE
EST AISEE
1924
Evening dress with slender fitting gold bodice
and full pink taffeta skirt.
André Marty
Gazette du Bon Ton

35

NUBIENNE
c. 1924
Gold lamé evening gown
supported by an amethyst necklace.
Art, Goût, Beauté

36

SOLDAT
1924
White woollen suit with 'pocket'
designs embroidered in blue and red.
Art, Goût, Beauté

37

1924
FAUNE
Dress of black pleated taffeta.
FLORENCE
Dress of brick coloured rep
embroidered with silver thread.
Art, Goût, Beauté

38

1925
Three day dresses.
Supplement, *Art, Goût, Beauté*

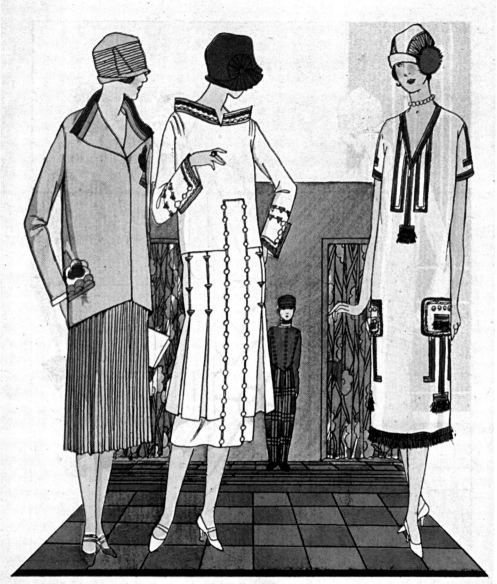

Créations Paul Poiret

39

ROBE DE JARDIN
1926
White crêpe de Chine dress
with hand-painted designs.
Art, Goût, Beauté

40

NIAGARA
1926
Dancing dress of 'Silver Rain',
a pleated A.G.B. fabric.
Art, Goût, Beauté